“Behi

Behind The Dollar

Summer Cooper

"Behind the Dollar"

Dedication

I would like to dedicate this book to Reggie Cooper Jr my little brother and my dear sister Jessica Cooper. The amount of love, adoration, appreciation and respect I have for her is something that I can't put into words. I would also like the state of Florida to have a better look at my sister's case because she's a non-violent person. All I want is for her to get the help that she really needs. Jessica, this one is for you!

Acknowledgment

I would like to thank everyone who helped me write this book, especially Dave, Cochran, Elizabeth, April, Laura, Clarie, Alexander, Rebecca, Merrit, Layna, Kignt, Gina, Paul and my parents for always being there for me and supporting me through thick and thin. I love you guys.

CONTENTS

About the Author

Summer cooper is an entrepreneur who was born and raised in central Florida. She was born in a small town but quickly moved into the big lights of cities around the country. She is a creative person who has always had a passion for animals and made her way in life as an adult entertainer for twenty-two years. Her book tells the story of what it was like to make a living in the industry. She is a barrel racer and loves the sport of rodeo, and her story will tell you how she does it all.

"Behind the Dollar"

Chapter 1: Broken Childhood

My name is Summer Cooper, and this is where my story begins. I am 45 years old now and would like to take you along as I reflect on my life and share my journey. It's a pity that, as far as I can remember, my life has never been normal, not even as a little girl. My early childhood was not an ideal one. I believe kids should have a carefree life full of fun, happiness, and love. However, I can't relate to that. I have an elder sister, and I am the youngest. I guess having a sister made things a little better at times.

When my parents were together, we didn't have much of a family life or spend quality time. Even as a child, I could always sense the friction between my parents and wondered what was wrong since they argued a lot. If I were to carefully pick and select one aspect of my childhood that I was very grateful for, it would be that we always had animals at our house. My dad had a bluetick coonhound dog named Blue, and he stayed inside with us. I was fond of all animals, but I loved horses the most.

There was just something about them. I remember being so fascinated by their lengthy, thick, silky manes, long necks, the structure of their muscular bodies, and how majestic they appeared to be. So, to say that I was on cloud nine when I got my first pony would be an understatement. I named her Lollypop, and I had her when my parents were still together. She was a paint-color pony and was the cutest, sweetest, and most obedient little girl ever. Her expressive baby-blue eyes could capture the entire world, and her blonde mane was as smooth as silk.

When I first laid my eyes on her, I thought God had really spent a good amount of time creating her. he was undeniably perfect in every way. Lollypop and I became attached in the blinking of an eye. You know how they say animals can sense touch and vibes quickly; I guess she felt my love for her from day one. In fact, she was the coolness of my eyes; spending time with her, playing, and taking care of her gave me a lot of satisfaction and fulfillment. During my time with her, I would forget everything that was happening in my life, and it simply became background noise. Lollypop was a very loving pony; she could tell when I was feeling down and would come put her head around my neck to show affection.

And to tell you the truth, this act of hers would melt me to the core and would fascinate me so much. As far as schooling is concerned, I went to kindergarten twice and dressed as a tomboy. I wasn't into those girly dresses and liked to wear western clothes such as jeans and a T-shirt. That was my style at the time. Things between my parents were still quite unstable, and soon they were going through a rough divorce.

As a kid, seeing your parents argue and fight can severely impact you, and I speak from personal experience. Needless to say, my mental and emotional health was compromised during that time, and I vividly remember having these mixed, confused, and unsettling thoughts and emotions. I had multiple questions in my head that I didn't get answers to and was disturbed. I mostly wanted to stay with my dad since I was closer to him and felt like he was my safe place.

However, in the beginning, I only stayed with him on the weekends. I used to look forward to the weekends since that was the highlight of my entire week. My dad and I had a good relationship. We used to watch Mr. Ed, which was my favorite show, I played a lot of games, and we had a meaningful time together. I was about 12-13 years old when my elder sister Jessica got pregnant at the age of 15. My mom was furious about it, and my sister moved out of my mom's house and started living with my aunt.

Mom and Jessica used to fight and scream all the time, and it caused a lot of disturbance in the environment of the house. After my parents got divorced, my dad bought me another pony, and it was also a paint. His name was Cherokee, and I had him before I started Jr. Rodeo. I lived with my dad from the age of 13 to 14, and the best thing that happened to me was that he got me started in Junior Rodeo, knowing my love for horses. I thoroughly loved it and started on a horse named Big Brother, and he was just something else.

Me and my horse Big Brother

As my interest in rodeo increased, my dad bought me a gray horse whose name was also Blue. I used to do barrel racing, pole bending, and steer on decorating, and we did this for a few years. Living with my dad was excellent, and I rode horses every weekend until my dad met a woman, and little did I know that my life was soon going to take a turn for the worst. One afternoon, she showed up at Junior. Rodeo and my aunt were there with my mom.

In a matter of some time, things between that young woman and my dad became serious, and they ended up getting married. She could not stand my sister and me, and gradually the quality time with my dad was reduced to the extent that it eventually faded away.

Me and my horse Blue

That witch had managed to take my dad away from me. I remember one day I got off school and was on my way to the place where we kept the horses. I used to go there daily, and to my surprise, everything had gone up in smoke one day. There were no horses, the gates were open, and even the horse trailer was gone.

The horrible part was that there was no explanation

for this incident, and I sat there in dismay, crying a river until my dad picked me up. That was a day I felt like everything was over, and I knew that my dad's bride was behind all this, yet I stayed quiet. From there on, I started changing; I would miss school, wait behind the bushes until the bus went away, go inside the house when my dad left for work, and on the days, he would drive me to school, he would always smoke cigarettes. When I would reach school, my friends could smell it. I was in middle school at the time, and the friend group I had are still my friends to the due date.

Me and Leslie

Leslie was a new girl in town, and her mom was incredibly sneaky. She used to spy on us and read the letters we used to write to each other. Leslie and I were attached to the hip, wrote a lot of notes to each other, stayed together all the time, and sneaked out to do things we weren't supposed to. Later, her mom died due to an overdose. Leslie and I used to sneak out a lot, but Heather and I used to take off in my dad's truck or grandma's car to go to parties. We would also sneak with older guys, and everyone knew us.

Me and Heather

It was pretty unfortunate that my stepmom was so evil. She would use every chance she got to get me in trouble with my dad, and because of her lies, I suffered a few whippings from him. She and I have even had a fistfight in my room while my dad watched from the living room. I remember using my bebe gun to defend myself. Once, she took a picture of Heather and me next to the new Lincoln Mark Eight, which my dad had bought for her, and decided to frame us. We later found out that she had developed and mailed it to him, making it look like someone took this pic at a party we were at, and she sent it to him.

It was already beside her car at my house; she lied. No matter how much I tried explaining my truth, my dad didn't take a second to whip me for something I didn't do. She always won, and I was no match for her. It was so convenient for her to take me out like a piece of trash. She would go to every extreme to make me look like a bad person. Heather and I were not perfect, but I loved my dad, and she did every possible thing to put a gap between us. I then lived with my aunt, who had three kids, and it was more like family with her. She and my uncle were so cool; they cooked and also took us to school.

By that time, I was in 9th grade, and although living with my aunt and uncle was pleasant, I used to be confused and sad most of the time. My sister would come to pick me up for lunch, and I wouldn't go back. Not to mention, she also had a baby by that time. Some time passed, and my mom married another man that lived in Winter Haven, Florida, so I moved there. My mom and stepdad lived on a golf course; he had two kids who were in college. I found it strange that my mom always seemed to be embarrassed by us.

I started school over there, which was short-lived as I didn't care about it, and eventually, I was a dropout. In school, I made one friend who had an older boyfriend, and I was later introduced to another guy who was also older. At the age of 15, I used to sneak out of my window, and he used to come to pick me up. Since my mom kicked me out of the house, I started living with a guy named Chris, who drank a lot and was mean and abusive. He used to beat me up every time he drank, and I felt terrible knowing that both my parents knew exactly what was going on. At times I used to wonder why I had such a broken childhood.

Sure, my dad was influenced by my stepmother, but my birth mother worked close by the house I was living in. A reoccurring thought I had was why my mom didn't come to visit me. For most girls, sweet sixteen is something they desperately look forward to because of its hype. But, my sixteenth year was one that still haunts me even today. When I turned sixteen, my dad got me a car, but later, he took it away. My sister only came to see me when Chris wasn't home since he wouldn't let me see anyone and locked me in the house.

I can recall sitting on the floor behind the door while my dad would beg me to come out. However, that guy was ruthless and didn't let me see my dad. After some time, we went to live with his mom, who was a very nice lady. She told me that her son's anger issues have gone on his dad, who was in prison for stabbing his pregnant girlfriend. Sometimes, I used to question myself about what wrong I had done to receive a life like this, but you know how they say there is always a light at the end of a dark tunnel. You just have to keep your focus on the positive and look beyond the adversities.

One night my sister came in the middle of the night, loaded all my stuff, and took me to my mom's house. This was the night of my freedom, and I was so grateful to her for coming to my rescue. Getting out of there was truly a breath of fresh air, and the chains on my body felt uncuffed. I took a deep breath after getting out of that prison and heaved a sigh of relief. I then settled at my mom's house for a short period of time; my grandparents adopted my sister's baby during the first year only, so she went on with her life.

Jessica had a good job and started seeing a new guy with whom she also had another baby. During that time, I was also growing up and had a few small jobs at a drug store and then at the dry cleaners. My dad got me a purple mustang, but I didn't use it for too long since I had an accident. However, my mom's husband was kind enough to let me make payments on his son's old car, and I literally drove the wheels off of it. My mom later divorced this man and re-married my late stepdad. He was and still is the greatest man I know. He was so accepting of our crazy family.

Chapter 2: Finding my way

My early teenage years were also rough and traumatizing, just like my childhood. I am one to believe that your teens are very crucial, and it can be a confusing time in your life because of all the physical, emotional, mental, and social changes that you go through. Not to mention, this is a time when you are trying to define who you are, your beliefs, the dreams and goals you have, and so forth. On top of that, if your early life has been troublesome, it can be far more complex.

Regardless of whatever was happening in my life, I was getting by each day. I was still very young and was trying to find my way through life. It seemed as if I had to do it all alone. When I turned eighteen, I decided to get a job at a well-known restaurant called Hooters. It was a nice-looking place, and I felt like I would be a good fit here. My job description was simple; I worked as a waitress and served customers hot, delicious chicken wings. Luckily, most of the girls over there were friendly and welcoming.

I remember how they all loved wearing the small, bright orange shorts which were part of our uniform. I have to say, working at that restaurant really made me feel like I was at home. I thoroughly enjoyed my time there, and it felt like a much-needed break. I quickly became a customer favorite. I got along with the other girls pretty well, and in no time, we all became close to each other. The best part was that they were all so supportive and encouraging, knew how to uplift one another, and we were one big family. I was good at my job; the customers loved me, and I even met some girls that became my best friends.

As time passed, I grew as an individual and learned so much from my daily interactions with people. Fortunately, after a few weeks, I had made so much money and had my own apartment, which felt like I was living a dream. It wasn't huge in size but spacious enough for my need. My apartment really changed things for me; it gave me a new life, confidence, security, independence, and freedom. I was able to live freely on my own terms, didn't have anyone to fear or chaos, didn't have to deal with my parents/step-parents, and was definitely breathing on fresher grounds. I noticed that there was also a visible change in my mood, mental health, and personality.

As a matter of fact, I started feeling happy and content; I thought I was born to do this. I still vividly remember how amazing it felt to slowly and gradually set up my apartment, buy new furniture and decorate it with things and colors that I loved. My favorite part of the apartment was the lounge since its center wall covered an absolutely breathtaking oil painting of a horse. Soon as I would enter, my eyes would lay on it and remind me of my love for horses. Life seemed to be headed in the right direction.

I was proud of myself for accomplishing all this in such a short period of time. One fine afternoon, an old man came into the restaurant and had a polaroid camera wanting pictures of the girls; he was probably fond of photography. He sat at the biggest table we had and ordered a beer. Since none of the girls wanted to attend to him, I decided to go and take his order. Little did I know that this act of kindness would change my whole life forever.

We talked during my entire shift, and I discovered so much about him and his life. It turned out that he was very lonely and needed someone to talk to. Since I attended to him when no one else wanted to and gave him my precious time, he generously gave me a $400 tip which was insane. At first, it felt like it was a joke, but it wasn't. The next day he came in with a newspaper, sat in the corner, and of course, I went to take his order. We sat together and talked about different things, and while flipping the newspaper, there was an advertisement for a new dealership that had just opened in town.

There was a beautiful white Toyota Landcruiser on the front page for almost 60k. Upon looking at it, I remarked how nice it was, and without any second thoughts, he asked me if I wanted it, to which I immediately said yes. At that point, I didn't think he would actually get me the car, and I was quite casual about it. However, I was wrong because right after I expressed my desire of wanting it, he asked me for my phone number and told me that he'd call me tomorrow and we would go buy that car from the same dealership.

We didn't have cell phones back then, so I gave him my mom's number and went to her place to wait on the call. My sister was there, so I told her about it, and soon as the clock ticked three, Mike called and said, "Hey Summer, do you still want that truck?" while giggling, my sister and I said, "Oh yeah." Shortly after, we met him at the dealership; he spoke to the salesman, went to the bank, and came back with a cashier's cheque and bought me the car. After becoming the owner of such a fantastic car, I was over the moon.

I thanked Mike and went back to my mom's house. On the way back, my sister and I had the sunroof opened, loud music playing; and it honestly felt like it was too good to be true, but we made sure to enjoy every bit of it. After all, it's not every day that someone buys you a luxury car like that. I, of course, continued to work, and Mike would show up at my shift every day, bragging about how he bought me this car, and all the girls were so jealous of me.

My sister and I

As funny as it may seem now, I liked all the attention I was getting and wanted to stay in the limelight. Over the next six months, he had spent at least a million dollars on me. I was also helping my family. He even bought me, and three other girls boob jobs on my asking; my sister was one of them. In fact, she lived the experience with me. My sister was and still is my best friend. But she was struggling with drugs on and off and using them as recreation at that point.

Anyways, I was growing up and wanted to have a banging body let alone show it. By that time, I was smart enough to realize the appeal of a woman and began grooming and working on myself. Not to mention, with time, my sense of style and dressing also evolved. I was now into more feminine yet sexy clothing that showed my skin. I worked at Hooters for a year and was later fired without any reason, but I didn't care since I was meeting Mike every day at the malls, jewelry stores, and a new apartment on the lake; he bought me another car and whatnot.

I was living a carefree life full of luxury, and it may be unbelievable unless you lived it with me. Soon, I became a small-town celebrity; everyone knew me. I was taking care of everyone around me. I can recall my cell phone bill being 1k; it was crazy. It had only been a month since they first came out. Mike was a generous and great man, he continued to gift me things for a year, and to the best of my knowledge, I splashed a million dollars. However, do you know how they say that all good things must come to an end? The same happened to me.

Mike was old, and later, he passed away, so it all came down to the expensive cars and other things that I purchased at only 18-19 years of age. Eventually, I sold them and moved back with my mom. I want to point out that going through and becoming used to that kind of big money at such a young age was highly devasting when I didn't have it anymore. I was accustomed to a luxury lifestyle, and readjusting to my old life was tough, to say the least. I missed the life I lived with Mike and the things I got to experience.

Chapter 3: Night Lights

Things definitely changed after Mike's passing and brought forth several realizations. Although I knew that Mike was old and would eventually pass away, I guess I didn't expect it to be so soon. Or maybe, I got lost in my own new world to realize how fast time flew by. Nevertheless, death can be so scary, nerve-wracking, and sometimes even sudden. It makes us stop in time and reflect on how short life truly is. During the time I spent with Mike, I not only got to know him personally, but I also became used to him and all the luxuries he was providing me.

He became my go-to person for a lot of things, someone I could easily and blindly depend upon. Having someone you can rely on is a blessing. After his death, I faced the reality of life, and it felt as if my bubble of luxury and happiness had burst. Moving back in with my mom was not the best or ideal situation, but I knew I had to keep a roof over my head. I was still young, figuring out my life and dealing with a major loss. Living with my mom again was okay, and I got through it since I didn't have any other choice at the time. I was still friends with a girl I waitressed alongside, and we would talk and hang out occasionally.

She told me how she started dancing in Tampa at night and made $1000 per night. I was amazed, to say the least. As a matter of fact, the way she described her time over there made me think as if it was too good to be true, but some part of me was still intrigued to know more about it. Needless to say, it was pretty easy for her to talk me into going with her one day since she saw the curiosity in me to look into what she was doing to make some good money. Since I no longer had a car, she picked me up one night to come and see the club. I had my doubts and apprehensions, but I can't deny the fact that I was excited.

I decided to get ready a whole hour before she was supposed to come to pick me up. I wanted to clean myself up and look pretty. After all, I couldn't mope around and sit in the house doing nothing all day. Life never stops for anyone. So, I put on a beautiful satin black sleeveless body con dress with a thigh-high slit on the right side, threw on a pair of Christian Louboutin red heels, and paired the dress with minimalistic gold accessories and curled my hair halfway down to add that extra volume and bounce.

For my makeup, I ensured to keep it soft and shift the focus on my lips by applying a bright blood-red lip gloss on them. While growing up, I was well aware of the attraction behind red lips and how they exude confidence and boldness. Not to mention, I showered in an expensive Tom Ford perfume that Mike had gifted me before his passing. I remember how he said this was a best-selling popular fragrance amongst elite women, and the perfume a woman wears says a lot about her. More say, a well-perfumed woman is deadly enough to catch a man.

Those words really spoke and stuck with me, so I followed through. I was eager to see where my friend danced and judge the place itself, but the nervousness factor was still present. She picked me up at the time she had given, and we drove off. As I stepped out of the car and laid my eyes on the nightclub, my very first impression was how fancy this place looked on the outside, and the traffic was enough to say it would be packed inside. My friend had a pass since she was one of the dancers here, so we didn't have to wait in the long queue. I was taken aback as soon as I got inside; my jaw literally dropped, and my pupils enlarged.

I honestly felt like I had been transported into a whole other world. That nightclub was absolutely insane! Everything was undeniably spectacular, from the lavish interior, the class of the people present, the DJ, the music, and the ambiance to the lights and design. Just a few seconds later, my eyes met a huge pole dancing stage. This was it; the girl I waitressed with wasn't lying one bit when she described this place. However, it was at that moment that it hit me that she wasn't just any regular dancer; she was specifically working there as a strip dancer. No wonder she was making that kind of money on a nightly basis and maybe even more than what she had told me.

So many questions ran through my mind, such as how she even got into this profession, who trained her, who groomed her, and so forth. While I was present there, I managed to learn and pick up on a lot from a single visit. Women were using their beauty and their bodies to make money through strip dancing. As old as it can get, the men over there were all in awe of the dancers and would happily splash thousands of dollars for a good show. As far as I heard, some would even have long-term affairs with the dancers spoiling them at their finest.

And why would they not? They were a sight for sore eyes, and their dancing bodies did all the talking. As I recall my first time there, I noticed how the men in that crowd eyed me even though I wore more clothes than any of the strip dancers. I was always told that my looks could kill, and that's when I believed the authenticity of that statement. I guess they wanted to get to know me and watch me under the clothes and on the grand stage. Men will always be men, you know. That was a night to remember, indeed, and when I saw my friend do her thing, I thought I could do it too. After all, I was confident in my own skin and could also really use the money for many things.

Fast forward, it didn't take too much time until she started picking me up, and we would go dancing in Tampa. In fact, I was actually really great at strip dancing, and to my surprise, it came to me very naturally. My body would seamlessly pick up and dance to the rhythm of the music, and the hidden sexy girl would unleash herself. Not to mention, I rocked the role, and my moves turned heads left, right, and center. I personally think that everything you do in life is an art and a form of expression. I expressed myself through dance and music and really enjoyed myself.

My early dancing days in early 2000

There was something so sexy about wearing different lingerie, swaying my hips, getting on the pole, dancing my heart out, and undressing for the entire crowd. I have to admit, at first, it can be a little awkward, but I got the hang of it pretty quickly. I was on cloud nine when I made my first

$1300. It was insane how you could make so much money through strip dancing, and the way the men would cheer and put dibs on me would surely increase my self-esteem and popularity.

When I first started dancing

All it took was a couple of performances, and I had decided what I wanted to do in life. Therefore, I proceeded to pursue my dancing career. In fact, I believe I was born to perform. As I took the stage, I made sure to be the center of everyone's attention. I acted fast. I was a true professional, used my eyes to speak a thousand words, and let my body entice and lure the toughest of men, making them weak in the knees.

I knew exactly what my body was capable of and used that to its full advantage. Some of the other dancers would even analyze and ask me for tips on how to be like me. I looked the part every single night. I tipped staff very well and got to where I never went on stage unless big money was involved.

My looks when I started dancing

I would tip the DJ 100$ on the down low to miss my stage sets so I could work the floor more. In fact, I also always tipped managers a lot, so I could come and go as I wanted. It wasn't always easy to give good tips, but I had to look at the bigger picture. I was typically the latest to arrive at work. My scheme was good since all the other girls got there early and would be tired or had too much to drink. On the contrary, I was fresh walking in, always ready, so I wasted no time having to primp in the back before hitting the floor.

Sometimes I would leave one club at closing and go to another one that would be open till 6 am. Most girls' feet were hurting from being there since 7 pm. But when I showed up at midnight, I never lost. While they sat on the chairs talking with friends, I would ask every guy for a dance. Rejection could never kill my confidence. On what seemed to be a slow night, I would pace myself and make it a game. I would do five dances an hour gives me $100. At that time, they were 20 where I was working, so every hour, I'll make 100. By the time I left, I would have 800 if I stayed an 8-hour shift.

I used my singles to tip out. I never went in expecting anything I knew what I was making was more than the average. 'Slow and steady gets the prize' was something I lived according to what my banker always told me. I am a very patient person. Remember, I was way ahead of every girl already. Before they were old enough to dance, I had already experienced a lavish life. So, to this day have always been very humble. I soon started to save money to buy a car, but my dreams came crashing down when my friend's boyfriend stole my money since he knew where I was hiding it.

That was a lesson well learned, and I became more careful. Fortunately, within a month, I had made my name in the nightclub and started making a good amount of money. I was always the most well-dressed and drove the nicest cars. The word about me traveled fast around Tampa, and my friend had been telling other girls about when I worked at Hooters and how an old man had spent a million on me. Every pimp in town was coming to the club trying to pull me. I then met another guy named Kurt, who was a customer, and shared my story with him.

Luckily, he was all about me and loved to show me off, let alone spoil me with expensive gifts. He would give me and another girl money to come to his house parties. Kurt would set up a personal shopper at Sak's 5th Ave for me, and I would be dressed in Gucci from top to bottom. Kurt even paid my house rent for a year, bought me a presidential Rolex, took me to New York, surprised me at work with a Mercedes, and was crazy about me. I finally went on a date with Troy, one of the biggest pimps in town that had the prettiest girls, and yes, his girls became seemingly jealous of me. We ended up staying in the same luxury apartment complex.

Mercedes that Kurt bought me and delivered to the club

On the nights he would stay with me, one of the girls would sit outside my apartment because she was almost obsessed with me. Troy split his time between both of our apartments, and Kurt was not a pimp.

In fact, he lived in Orlando, and I met him just before I got with Troy. However, one of Troy's other girls wanted to hang out with me so bad I would have Kurt give Troy 1k a night for her to go to his house parties with me. The only way we were ever allowed to miss work was if we each made 1k a night, so Kurt would pay that just to spend time with me.

Later that girl and I became close and decided to leave Troy. But Kurt was still in the picture; he continued to spoil me with gifts, sent limos to pick up my friends and me to attend his Orlando parties, and even took me to my first football match. And that wasn't it; he even paid $5000 to have my name on the scoreboard during halftime.

Score board at the opening game of the new buccaneer's stadium

Anyway, fast forward; Troy's girls wanted to leave with me, so I helped them and assisted them in stashing away money without him knowing. I had fun for a while but decided that life wasn't for me. I was making such lavish money, and I wasn't giving it to anyone anymore. Time passed, and I eventually had a fallout with Kurt. Plus, there were more people lining up on me. The other girl that left Troy started to drift apart and got into drugs. I, on the other hand, stayed and made money. My life was good, and I was living it up, working hard for my money, and trying to stay focused on my goals. I wasn’t going to let any distractions come my way.

Chapter 4: Heartbreak

Life was good, or I would say a better way to express it would be that I finally had the right amount of stability. Stability in life is crucial, and we all search for it. After all my hard work, undying dedication to my career, and focus on my goals, I was now enjoying the fruit of my labor. I fully understand that it's imperative to work hard, save and plan for your future but taking out time to unwind is equally necessary.

By this time, I had done and saved up enough to go on a long and much-needed break. And I thought to myself, what better way to relax than to travel? I was always someone who had the desire to see the world, learn about various cultures, explore new places, and try out different cuisines and recreational activities. Safe to say, this was my calling. I had the money and could also afford to take a short break and also explore other work opportunities during my travel.

I wasted no time and decided to take the first flight to Miami. Miami was one of those cities that I was impatiently, or I should say, dying to go to. It's famous for its pristine beaches, non-stop nightlife, mind-blowing skyline, luxurious shopping malls, architecture, high-end hotels, and whatnot. For the time that I was there, I ensured to go to a few of the most popular beaches like South Beach, stayed at a five-star hotel, ate finger-licking good meals, and shopped till I dropped. Even though I was somewhat on vacation, I had work somewhere at the back of my mind.

During my mall visits, I had so much fun shopping and bought these jaw-dropping, undeniably sexy pieces of clothing that I was sure I'd rock. I was extremely experimental with my looks and strived to look outstanding every time. I was firm on the belief that looking good is a lifestyle, and one has to go to all lengths to maintain it. I stayed in Miami for a few days and then headed off to New Orleans. The thing I was most excited about in this city was the crazy nightlife and music. As a matter of fact, I remember doing a spontaneous performance at one of its most popular clubs. I was lucky to have a huge network and a name for myself.

One of the managers there knew about me through someone and allowed me the liberty to own the stage. Although my travel was not for work, I couldn't miss the opportunity and went for it. Staying and exploring New Orleans was a true delight. Safe to say, the next on my list was Memphis and Las Vegas, which were also insane. Traveling really made me realize how alive and refreshed I felt. Fortunately, money was a thing that came to me easily, as some would say. I flew there to work and made it a habit of flying to Memphis, Vegas, and New Orleans to work. Memphis was a place I would fly into on a Friday night and leave on Sunday. Two nights in that club would bring 3-4k.

The dances there were $40 each, whereas other clubs were offering $20. After making a good amount of money from my work trips, I was back and more energized than ever. I had no idea what was in store for me, and it all dates back to the Super Bowl 2001. I met a pro athlete that week who played in Texas, and he was going to be in town all week. I made more money than I could count; I hung out with him every day and worked at night. Soon, he became someone that I had been seeing for years. He would happily fly me all over; he partied and knew how to have fun.

I then moved to Miami, and he would fly there and stay with me, which was super sweet. He even paid for every trip of mine; he was such a fun person and showed me a whole new side of things. Some time passed, and I started dating another pro athlete from Miami who played in Ohio. Thus, I would fly back and forth all the time. Although he never paid me nightly, he flew me first class and bought me the finest jewelry gifts. It didn't just end there; he would stay with me at his house in North Miami beach on his days off. We became very close after a few years, but my friend was still on the sidelines.

I think my guy knew about him, and one Sunday, they played against each other, both defense linemen. (My old friend Dallas and my new one Roy.) The day the two boys played against each other was truly a day to remember. I was watching them on TV, and I remember being so nervous. The All-Star game was in Philly, and as far as I recall, he asked to fly me out. Therefore, I brought my sister and told Roy I was going to Tampa to see my family, and little did I know that he had the password to my voicemail. After I boarded the flight, Dallas left a voice message instructing me where the limo would be picking me up from.

Oh boy!

My phone was blowing up just when I landed, and Roy was pissed. I then told Dallas that he had to get me on the next flight to Miami. Shortly after that, my sister and I went back to my place in Aventura, and it wasn't long until Roy showed up. I knew things would get pretty heated and wasn't looking forward to it. That night was surely one to remember. Roy and I got so toxic from that point, but the irony was that Roy and I couldn't get enough of each other, and we stayed together for four years. At the time, I worked at one of the biggest clubs in Miami, and that's where I met Tif.

I was glad to meet her; she was dating a player from down there, and we instantly became friends. As a matter of fact, we are still best friends. Tif danced at other clubs, she would see Roy and call me, and I would leave work and barge at other clubs to fight other girls. My relationship with Roy was extremely toxic and unhealthy. Years went by, and man after man came into my life, but Roy was the one who I would stay with over anything. I danced in Miami for four years, and Roy and I would have the biggest fights. Eventually, they got so bad that my mom would get involved. One day, my mom finally said no more. She stood up for me and told him that she would call his coach if he ever called me again, and things would get ugly.

Unfortunately, I was in the hospital at the time because I swallowed 90 Xanax pills over a fight because I wanted to escape. I knew it was time to distance myself from Roy since I could no longer let an unhealthy, mentally, and emotionally destructive relationship rule over me. I had to think long-term and focus on the bigger picture. Sure, it was very difficult, but this decision was one that had to be made at any cost. I moved to Lakeland, which was close to Tampa, and was back with my mom. My relationship with Dallas fell apart when his wife found his phone bills and other information leading to the fact that we had been friends for a long time.

I didn't even know he was married. I never heard from him again after that, in addition to me being a traveling dancer. I would meet many men who would eventually start flying me back out and paying for my stay. Back then, you couldn't just walk into a club in Vegas and get hired. The club I used to work at is now Crazy Horse 2, and the girls had to audition. However, as for me, never in my 22 years did I have to do that. I was well-spoken and knew how to take care of people.

Another thing I would like to mention is that in Vegas, I had no problems as I met a guy in Miami that was very well-connected, and I went in the back door and right to work. Your money there was based on class and how much you took care of the guy running it. Men with big money had a special door and would decide what girls they brought back to entertain them. I was always a pick; I didn't drink at work but sold bottles and took very good care of the staff. I mean, if you are making 1k off one guy, throw the guys 200 to secure your place there.

That's the logical thing to do. Greedy girls didn't make solid money. In other clubs, where you may spend a 100 to work all night, including the tips, I would spend 3-500 depending on the night I had. Even on bad nights, I took care of the right people. It was a very tight program there. They could easily tell you to leave if you were making a lot and not taking care of the right staff. However, I didn't face any such issue because I always played it smart and steered clear of getting into trouble or tarnishing my image.

My well-connected friend I met in Miami

I believe it's essential to keep your head in the game and not get distracted or overlook the things that matter. Regardless of which profession you're in, you must have an eagle-eye focus and make planned moves to position yourself for success and avoid unnecessary drama and issues.

Chapter 5: Living A Dream

Each one of us wishes to live our dreams and enjoy everything we have ever wanted. Luckily, I was one of those people who got the golden opportunity to live my life-long dream. I was rodeoing, riding horses, dancing, making money, and overall, really happy with where I was in life. But before I get into all those nitty-gritty details, let's go back in time from where it all began. I decided to move back to Tampa in 2004 with my mom, and safe to say it wasn't a wrong decision.

In August 2005, I drove to Waco, Texas, for a barrel race just a few days before hurricane Katrina was expected to hit. If I were to describe the barrel race experience in Waco in just one word, I would say it was absolutely amazing. There were all kinds of gorgeous horses, the spirits were high, people were excitedly participating, and I was over the moon to be a part of it.

However, once the storm hit, they closed 1-10, so naturally, my route home wasn't going to be closer for potentially two weeks. Therefore, I was stuck and forced to stay in Texas until things got better. I believe everything in life happens for a reason, even if you can't see the good in that particular moment. Anyways, I decided to make the most of my time there.

Given my friendly nature and personality, I managed to make some friends who owned a ranch, and I could keep my horses there. Other than spending time with horses, I knew I had to continue working, so after a few days, I decided to look up some clubs and landed at a club called New Orleans Nights, which is actually closed now. I was a professional, always put my best foot forward, and was ready to bring my A-game wherever I went.

After successfully landing a position at the club, I quickly fit in, began making money like always, and even met a guy who gave me a fuel card from his company along with a pin number. I used that for a year until it expired, and that is how I paid for all my fuel rodeoing and my friend's fuel. In fact, I was known to be very generous. I had a living quarters horse trailer at the time, so after work at night, I would quietly go back to the ranch before anyone woke, took care of my horses, and climb back in bed. No one ever knew I was dancing. Shortly before I thought of driving back to Florida, one of my dearest friends, Paul, called me and asked how far I was from Sulphur Springs, Texas.

He told me he knew someone who wanted to sell five acres of land and that I should go check it out. Paul's suggestion seemed nice; I thought there was no harm in visiting the property since my living condition could be better than the current one. Even though I enjoyed living in my horse trailer, it was like a house. I didn't like sneaking in at night from dancing. To my surprise, I immediately saw myself living there as soon as I laid my eyes on the property.

Honestly, it was as if my whole life perfectly pieced together and flashed right before my eyes like I was watching a movie. Something about that place was so beautiful and serene. I was instantly sold! Although I'm not one to make hasty decisions, I didn't want to miss this fantastic opportunity. So, I called home and asked my stepdad for help. He even brought my mom and I closer the day they met. He was a genuine person, and there wasn't a hint of pretentious in him.

Without any questions, he agreed to finance it for me, and I put in the down payment. My stepdad and I developed a close relationship over time. He was such a sweet and nice person; he let me down and always trusted and supported me. I never knew a stepdad could be as awesome as him. Once the financial matters were done and dusted, things gradually started falling into place, and it was just the beginning of a new life for me.

My late step dad and I

I was so enthusiastic about decorating my new house and calling it home. I kept working and putting into the place until I got a big break at work on a Sunday. While most people from other professions relax and unwind on Sundays, it was the opposite for me. In fact, Sundays were considered to be 'money days.' Most girls were super tired from the weekend but still worked on a Sunday since it seemed like most men came out this day and had plenty of money to splash.

One fine Sunday, I danced for a guy named Fred; he was in love. From my experience, I learned if a guy came to the club on Sunday, he was ready to spend money. Therefore, I thought there was no harm in working on Sundays. We exchanged stories and started getting to know each other. I told him about my plans in life, how I got to Texas, the land I bought, and how I wanted to build a barn and fencing. Fred was quite impressed by my journey so far and thought I was the definition of a true career and goal-oriented woman. Honestly, it's nice to hear someone acknowledge and praise you for the things you've accomplished.

As we got to know more about each other, he told me he had just inherited close to a million dollars which was music to my ears. His parents had passed away; he was adopted and lonely and wanted to spend time with me and help me. He was a really great man. We didn't start slow, as he was crystal clear about his intentions. In fact, he took no time to send someone to build me a four-stall horse barn with a concrete center; he had built split rail cedar fencing and arranged an electric set up for me to put my horse trailer there.

Once this was all down, I moved my horses and trailer to the first piece of my land. I couldn't be happier. Things were aligning up pretty fast; we traded my truck for a new one, upgraded my living quarters trailer for one that was close to 100k, and started buying more horses starting from 20k to 80k. Soon, I had an impressive string of horses. At one point, I couldn't believe that I had collected so many horses. Looking at each of them filled my heart with pure bliss and peace. They were the apple of my eye. Anyways, all he and I were doing was spending money. Not to mention, I was living my best life because I was dancing so much and entering lots of barrel races/rodeos.

It's safe to say that I had the best of both worlds and didn't have to give up on anything. As far as Fred was concerned, it was a make-believe relationship to me and not sexual at all. But I would go to clubs with him and have all the girls show him affection which he loved. The thing that I had going on with Fred went on for two years. In addition to what he inherited; he was getting 250k every November for the next several years. Things between Fred and I lasted until he wanted more from me, which I wasn't willing to give.

Thus, I had to cut him off. While I know that this isn't the case for all men, but at some point, or the other, feelings come in between, and two people aren't on the same page in terms of that. In the past, when I was fifteen years old, I dealt with a lot of lack of true affection. My past at age 15 had a lot to do with the lack of true affection I showed everyone. When I was buying horses, I met a lady who was the go-to for top horses, and she made commissions. I started working with her, and eventually, we became good friends. Later, she introduced me to my ex-husband since she was married to his uncle in the past.

Chapter 6: Getting Married and Starting Over

Sometime after I was introduced to the man that later became my husband, he and I hit it off. He was a rancher, and I finally connected with someone that had the same interest as me, such as horses, rodeo, and dogs. It felt good to connect with a like-minded person. Not to mention, he was a humble man, so it seemed like a win-win situation. Things were looking good for our future, and we got engaged just after a few months of dating. I was in my early thirties at the time and thought maybe this was the change I needed.

I have to admit, during this time, I didn't give much thought to the fact that I was making an extremely huge amount of money and what I would do after marriage. Anyways, I took the plunge as it seemed right at the moment, and we got married in November. We got married in the presence of our loved ones and close family and friends. His mom married us at her breathtakingly beautiful ranch home; she was the judge.

My sister and I when she moved to Texas the first time when I was married

My mom, stepdad, and sister would fly out to Texas from Florida to be a part of everything. Seeing them take part in my wedding festivities made me feel so special and loved. After marriage, I moved in with him and ended up selling my place. It was great in the beginning, but I always stayed to myself.

His family was nice but always asked a lot of questions about my past and some of the expensive things I had. He had a lot of lands; I started to train and sell horses. In fact, I would bury myself in one horse particularly. I lost a horse in 07 to a very tragic event, so needless to say, I was going through a lot and decided to train my own horse instead of buying high-priced horses.

My sister and I on my wedding

Keeping that decision in mind, I set a goal of training a young horse and entering the BFA futurity for four-year-olds. I went to a well know Barrel racer and told him what I wanted to do. He was kind enough to show me a pen of three-year-olds, and I picked one that was tall, had a short tail, and just came off the race track. His name was Red Streak, and I immediately told the Barrel racer that I wanted him. Without a second thought, I paid him $6500, hauled him home, and immediately started training for his four-year-old year. I would ride him daily regardless of the freezing cold, rain, snow, or even the blazing hot summer days.

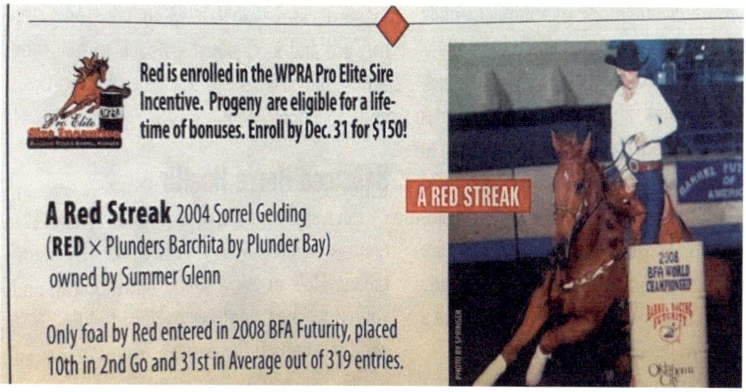

2008 BFA

December 2008 was our year, and I headed to Oklahoma City for the fraternity. During that time, my husband and I were not on such good terms, but I was determined to show off this hard work. Booboo and I spent the next week in the freezing cold in OKD. Round one – I was 15.9 – made a clean run, but it wasn't fast enough to secure my spot in the finals. Giving up was not an option, so I knew I had to try again and hopefully be successful the second time around. On the day of round two, I knew I had to be faster to make it to the finals.

My dog Boo-boo

The clock stopped at 15.661, and the guy I bought him from was at the end of the alleyway to high-five me. We did it, and I couldn't be happier! Some time passed, and things got better between my husband and I. But soon, his drinking habit caused me to become distant. I was never into such things and disliked them. Although he was never mean to me or anything, drinking was a huge turn-off for me. So, that became a problem in other areas as well. This was the very first time I had lived with a man since I was fifteen, and I used to get sexually abused by a man who drank and became violent with me.

Sexual abuse was one thing and violence another, so together, these two things really took a toll on me. I became very distant. Trauma is something that takes months or even years to get out of and recover. Its effects are skin-deep, and the wounds don't heal easily. The childhood trauma I experienced with a man was something that I had clearly not healed from. My dog Booboo who was nine years old at the time and was my safe place. I could just go and cuddle with her and feel better. There was something so special about our bond.

Not to mention, she could tell when I was upset and tried to cheer me up. She slept with me every night and soon in separate bedrooms from my husband. In all honesty, I was so lucky and grateful to have her by my side. I don't know what I would do without her. From the years 2009 to 2011, things were getting pretty tough for me; just adapting to marriage, not being able to be myself, and depression had started to get the better of me. I felt terrible and really struggled to navigate through those three things at once. My mom would come to visit me, and I remember every time I had to drive to the airport to drop her off would be so difficult.

I used to cry a river and didn't want her to leave because not having her around hurt so bad. During those few years of my marriage, I had been in Texas. My sister's drug addiction got really bad. I was sending her money on a nightly basis for the hotel, food, or anything else she needed. But the worst part was that deep down, I knew she was using that to buy drugs. I couldn't stop sending her money because hearing my sister say that she was sleeping in her car or staying hungry was something I couldn't imagine. She was my sister and best friend; how could I leave her like that?

She was struggling and going through a lot more than we saw on the surface level. I tried my best to be a good sister and stand with her as a strong support system. My sister's youngest daughter was being taken care of by my mom and step dad. We had to make these arrangements in order to ensure her child would not suffer. At this point, my sister had started shooting up meth, and honestly, my heart ached for her. I would fly home to visit, and on a very rare opportunity, I would get the privilege to see her.

My heart would break into a million tiny pieces thinking of her and seeing her in that terrible state. The drugs had changed my dear sister to a great extent. She was an insanely beautiful girl with clear blue eyes and an amazing body, but the drugs sucked the life out of her and left her withered like a flower. Unfortunately, it wasn't long until she ended up in prison for the first time. Needless to say, I hated it for her, but at the rate at which she was consuming drugs, she would end being dead. She did one year in state prison in Florida, but when she finally got out, my ex-husband and I moved her straight to Texas for a fresh new start. I believed that she should start over, give life another chance, and do better this time around.

Simultaneously, I also understood that it might take time, but I stayed positive and hoped for the best. I bought her a car when she arrived, my ex-husband set her up at a friend's ranch who had a guest house, and I even had a job waiting for her at an eye clinic. I really wanted to see her rise from the ashes, regroup, and change her life for the better. Things were good for a while, and my ex-husband's mom made some calls and got Jessica a job at a hospital in the emergency room. This was something Jessica was familiar with before she got into drugs. My sister worked at a large hospital in Tampa, Florida, and got experience there. She was always good in the medical field, and everyone loved her.

Soon, she enrolled in classes to become an RN. I was immensely proud and happy for her since her life was now moving toward normalcy. However, Jessica was still struggling with her body image; she had gained a lot of weight after she had left drugs. Some time passed, and my sister started going to a weight doctor who was prescribing her weight loss pills. Although she was successfully losing weight, something was off and odd. During that time, I started working in the night shift at the same hospital and was doing the same job my sister was doing during the day. To my surprise, the nurses shared and expressed their genuine concern about her and all the weight she was losing.

Additionally, I was also informed that she had been calling into work late, and that was quite unlike her. Naturally, I became alarmed and began thinking of reasons why there was a sudden change in her. She had also started becoming highly secretive, and the first obvious thought I had was that she was probably back on drugs. I hoped that I would be wrong, but the reality was that she was indeed back on drugs. Given her relapse, she didn't want me to see her in the same condition. Eventually, she lost her job at the hospital because of drugs, and it wasn't long until I quit.

Things back home weren't ideal for me, and I had solid reasons to quit. To shed some light on my situation, I was having problems at home and started spending time at a ranch that was not far from Sulphur Springs. It was a small town named Winnsboro, Texas. The same friend who introduced me to my ex-husband was the one who took me to this ranch. I discovered she had been selling horses to this guy for his daughter. At first, I was just going there to ride horses in his covered building. But little did I know that it would turn into something much more. We would talk for hours and hours, and we both fell really fast and hard for each other.

One thing I want to point out is that he was married for seventeen years and expressed how unhappy he was in his marriage. You know, time is not a measure of anything. He mentioned how his wife struggled with a pill addiction, so obviously, things were not good at his home. Since both of us were on the same page, we filed for divorce from our then-spouses. In a few short months, my divorce was final, and he built me a house on his land. However, his divorce was going to take over a year because he had kids that he loved dearly.

Additionally, he was also a wealthy man. I have to admit he and I were very close, and I fell in love. We would stick by each other through a lot of hard times during his divorce. I wanted to be his peace and someone he would turn to in times of sheer difficulty. At the time, I was barrel racing a lot, and he would show his support by buying me a few horses. In fact, he bought me a horse for 30k and another one for 65k. Despite the fact that we tried to keep everything down on the low, they started to get super public.

His ex-wife and my ex-husband would talk, and she found out that I used to dance. She looked down on me for it, but I didn’t care about it. My attention was on how he and I were in love, and love conquers all. Love is one of the most beautiful, fulfilling, and complete things to experience in this world. I had never had a connection with any man like I did with him. We were so attracted to each other. Anyways, a whole year went by, and unfortunately, his divorce got pretty nasty; I felt so much guilt and thought about all the pain that was caused. Therefore, I decided to go to Florida in order to let things cool down and clear my headspace. I feel like it’s necessary to take a break when your heart feels heavy and you need time to think things through.

We did some talking while I was gone, and the conclusion was to part ways. Even though things ended, he was generous and kind enough to take care of me financially for the next six months. While I can’t put the finger on it or state one particular reason, I started talking to my ex and returned to him, which didn’t last long, maybe a few months. I went back to him for a while, but the damage was already done. While I was with him for a few months, my dog Booboo fell really sick.

She was twelve at the time, and sadly I had to let her go. She loved my ex-husband, and we loved her together. Now that I look back, I feel like we were supposed to happen. We got the closure we needed. Later, I moved out of his place and went to a friend's place who was a fellow barrel racer. She and her mom were sweet enough to help me move out. Life had to move towards normalcy, and I started dancing again; it took me a few weeks to get my own place close to Dallas. In the meantime, my friend kept my horses, and I took my dogs. Luckily, I picked up the pace just like I had never been gone.

This was my comfort zone, the nightlife, and the people in it, and I was accepted for who I was. My ex-husband didn't want to accept my life before him. Therefore, it was hard for me to be myself without feeling judged by him and his whole family. I really had no one in his family that I could talk to besides his twin brother's wife. We got along quite well; she was very pretty, loved dogs, and was an understanding individual. I feel like in a relationship as serious as marriage or, in fact, any other relationship for that matter, it's imperative to feel secure in your partner's energy. When you feel secure, you can be yourself and not have to pretend or be fake just to be accepted. As I said previously, that was lacking in my marriage.

Chapter 7: Back in The Club-How I Started Over and Better Than Ever

After almost five years of being out of the clubs, I was back better than ever. In all honesty, it felt amazing because I actually missed the clubs, the dancing, the crowd cheering my name, and the busy routine that always kept me on my toes. Nevertheless, I also thoroughly enjoyed my time off. I knew I needed to relax, unwind and reset. During this time, I learned some valuable life-changing lessons, discovered a lot more about myself, and started listing goals I wanted to accomplish. I believe there is no age limit to achieving your goals.

You are constantly learning and growing as an individual, and your goals keep changing. To back it up a little, I had previously given up on everything and wasn't in the best place. I worked for all those years before getting married. I sold my property to move in on my ex-husband's property and walked away with nothing but this was by choice. In fact, my lawyer asked me why I decided not to take anything from my ex.

Usually, ex-wives are fighting big, ugly battles to get something or the other on their name after the marriage breaks down. However, that wasn't the case with me. The reason behind my decision was simple, my ex-husband worked really hard for the land and cows he had, he did so much for me while we were married, and I chose to sell my place and move in with him. I was never forced or anything, so it didn't make sense for me to demand ownership of his belongings. All I wanted was his happiness; I wanted him to be happy even if it wasn't with me, and that is enough proof of my sentiments for him. And to this day, I can safely and proudly say he was by far the greatest man in my life.

Our downfall was a result of a lack of communication, and we all know how communication is extremely important in any relationship. Thus, our relationship got ruined. After several years of different experiences and all sorts of exposure, I've come to realize that even when you let people go after a relationship ends, you can still wish them well. Hate is heavy and really unnecessary, so why keep it inside your heart or let it make you bitter? Instead, I personally believe you should focus on cherishing all the good things and time spent with that person. Anyways, I told my lawyer I only wanted 30k to put a down payment on a new truck, and that's what I got.

I had no intention of asking for anything else; I wasn't greedy or selfish. I didn't care about his money. I knew it wouldn't take long for me to regroup. However, I also knew I would never be in this situation again as I was depressed, and it was a lot of work. Speaking from personal experience, the effects of depression can really eat you up from the inside and swallow you whole. Depression is mentally, emotionally, and physically exhausting. Some days, it feels like a dark grey stormy cloud hovering over you. I

went from one life to a totally different one. Nevertheless, I was strong enough to heal and come back twice as stronger. Sometimes, I think a setback makes us feel as if we will never see the light again, and we fail to understand our own strengths. But, with time, patience, consistency, and goals, anything is possible. As for me, my motto was to rise from the ashes and start fresh. Life is what we make of it, and in the end, our choices define who we are. I didn't want to waste any precious time, so I returned to the club. The warm welcome and greetings I received took me straight to cloud nine. I also leased a breathtakingly beautiful home in Rockwall, TX, near Dallas, started working seven days a week, and was on the hunt for property.

Luckily, I had friends keeping my horses, and I still had a relationship with the bank. Thus, I had the backing to get a property in six months. I managed to save the money I needed to put down on a piece of property, and while I was on the hunt, I met a man named Dave in my first month. To my surprise, we instantly became very close; there was just an undeniable instant click.

In the blink of an eye, we became best friends and spent every day together. It was wholesome, and we never got bored of each other. Dave was so much fun; we laughed so hard he was good for my soul, and we were always together. Dave and I were very adventurous and indulged in various activities daily. We went to the casino, went to eat, shopped, and even flew to Florida and rented a car so we could drive back with my sister's dog. My sister was still on drugs and was facing prison for the second time. I had a very hard time facing all this because stress, anxiety, and worry engulfed me. I just wanted her to realize what she was doing to herself and break free of that toxicity.

My friend Dave and I

Dave himself was a recovering alcoholic, so he was very understanding. He was very supportive, never judged my sister for anything, and always provided an ear to listen to and a shoulder to cry on. Dave was very street-savvy and was up for anything; he used to come to the club every night I worked and filled my garter with $500 to $700. I would talk to him on and off all night since he was my best friend and confidant. I never hesitated to share anything with him, and our connection was as real as it gets.

Although it took a little time, I was back in the saddle again and bought a 100k car that Dave would cheer me at every step of the way. I remember once we took a drive to a casino shortly after I bought it and stopped at a small-town strip club, and showed love to the girls working there. Dave and I did everything together; he knew my story and goals and supported me throughout. Not once did he question my decisions or choices. In fact, he was a very supportive man overall; I couldn't have asked for a better friend than him. Some time passed, and luckily,

I found ten acres of land about an hour from Dallas. Although it was bare land, it spoke to me, and I immediately knew this was the one.I was absolutely sure that I wanted to live here, and I envisioned my life there in a matter of a few seconds. I had a clear mental picture of how things would fall into place, and my gut feeling fully backed up my decision. 3rd July 2014 is a very special date in my life as it marks the day I closed the deal and was over the moon. Thankfully, I still live there. This was a new beginning for me, and I was ever-ready to start a new chapter of my life.

I've always been super into fitness, but there was a time when I let go and ignored myself during depression. Now that I was back in the game, I decided to prioritize my health and listen to my body.

Therefore, I started working out with a trainer and was engrossed in this new lifestyle. I naturally always had a great body but became untouchable in the club thanks to working out. Along with my art, my body spoke volumes. In fact, it often did all the talking. I would hear my name in conversations where my fitness was compared to the other girls, which was definitely a major ego booster.

After all, I had worked really hard to maintain shape. I was the fittest girl in the club, and rightly so. I would have two trainers and was working out five days a week. I started attracting a lot of men. They would call out my name, willingly throw hefty cash at me, and share their personal phone numbers and other details. I was the apple of everyone's eye. When I came back better than ever, I truly learned that it's never too late to restart your life. No setback or obstacle is too big; even if others do, you should never give up on yourself.

Always have strong faith in your talents and capabilities and regain your power. Fortunately, things were going well for me, and after about a year, I moved clubs and began working around Dallas. My routine involved working at one club till it closed at 2 am, and then I would head to another and be there till 6 am.

I was insanely focused, constantly on the move and hardly took a day off until and unless high-rolling customers would offer me around $1k-1500k or even more for a night on the town. During this time, I had a few high-profile spenders in my pocket. I would meet up for dinner before work with a girl I met at the late-night club. Surprisingly, there were a lot of similarities between us. She moved around the club like me, she hustled like me, she was smart and pretty, and people would always confuse us being sisters.

Therefore, we started telling customers we were sisters to avoid any confusion. Her name was April, and coincidently my birthday was also in April. Soon we became really good friends, and this was the first time in my dancing career that I had made a real friend at work. The best part about our friendship was that she was not only a friend at work but also outside of work. We had a great bonding; we could hit each other up and hang out casually too. Otherwise, making friends in this industry is a difficult task because other girls see you as a competitor and may try to take away your limelight. April also got to work late and worked hard till the club closed. We always bought our way off stage since we didn't want to miss making money from doing a stage set. Our intellectual capability was also insane. I always gave the DJ $100 to skip me. April, who went by Tara in the club, was my new best friend and, fortunately, still is. April and I made some good money and always stayed motivated and on top of our game; we had each other's backs and lived an awesome life.

Another thing I admire about her is that she didn't let fame and fortune get to her head. She did not allow herself to get involved in the wrong activities, such as drinking, drugs, or unnecessary partying. Safe to say, she lived a pretty normal life; her priorities were in check, and she also cared for her health.

April and I

April stopped dancing somewhere around the same time as I did and opened up her own business. She was always a very driven individual and strived for the next best thing, given her farsighted mindset. We had all the right connections; if she needed a girl for a customer or I did, we would get each other. We were never bored at work and always knew how to have fun and enjoy ourselves. We also went through similar personal issues.

She and I both had a terrible breakup, and I was so thankful for her being by my side. She proved to be the best every step of the way through her words, actions and behavior. April felt like the warm sun that shines after a rainy day. She was there for me like no other friend was. As I mentioned earlier, it's hard to trust girls in the business so having April by my side was a huge sigh of relief, peace, and comfort. I could run to her in times of absolute dismay and vice versa. I believe friendships are highly essential in life.

Having genuine friends that you can truly, without a doubt, trust, rely on, confide in and share experiences with is a blessing indeed. The world is full of fake and twisted people, so my advice to you is if you find a real friend, keep them close and never let them go. You don't come across a genuine soul every now and then. It had taken me several years to get close to the girls I worked with. I'm now 37 years old and made a successful career in the clubs. To shed more light on April, she started dancing later in life; she was

30 and had two lovely kids. She's an exceptional mom, went to cosmetology school, and had planned to do hair when she quit dancing and did just that. I felt so proud and inspired watching April accomplish her goals.

My other friend Laura had the least amount of time in clubs and was ten years younger than me. Nonetheless, she and I could handle thousands in a night while doing the least amount of work. I guess we just had our own unique way of scoring big. Laura was also always by my side. I had several high-rolling customers that would take care of me if I left the club to hang out at their house, and I always had them write cheques to my friends. If any of my friends wanted to go, I always organized the night, ensuring everyone was taken care of.

That was just my personality. Not to mention, one customer, in particular, was my absolute favorite. He was a powerful man, and we met at his restaurant while Laura and I were enjoying a delicious meal there. Now that I recall it, I had an instant electrifying connection with him. Little did I know, he was one of Dallas' most influential and wealthy men. Eventually, he and I became very close, he would set Laura and me up with court-side seats to the mavricksbasketball game, and whatever I wanted, he made it happen. With time, our connection grew, and we were together every night. He was sweet enough to cover my night of work and anything else I needed.

In fact, I found him generous, too, since he would let my friends come over to his 15-million-dollar house if they had a bad night. With my approval, he would take care of everyone. There aren't many hospitable or generous people out there who let others come over to their house to relax, swim, eat or have wine. And this is not all; he would willingly also sign cheques for my friends and allow me to fill in the amount for the work they missed. Usually, it was around $1k-2500k; his kindness was out of this world.

Additionally, he and I always enjoyed ourselves to the fullest; even after everyone went back home, I stayed. I was very drawn to him; there was something about his energy, I was very comfortable with him, and he trusted me. Years flew by, and we had the same routine, but I always kept my feelings in check. It was hard for me to do so because I felt something different for him. Even though I was always the 'ring leader,' brought all the girls and ensured none of them caused him problems, I had a job to do. I always tried my best to keep him happy. Seeing a smile on his face made my heart smile.

I want to emphasize that I never fell for any customer as I did for him in all my years of dancing. His vibe was special, he was classy and powerful, and our alone time together was sincere and passionate. They say that all good things come to an end, and eventually, the spark between us faded. However, it was expected. I was nearing my journey as a dancer and was mentally changing. He's still one of the few close people in my life and has selflessly and tremendously helped me so much over the years. Although I still see him from time to time, I keep my feelings aside till the due date.

The way I see it, I don't want these feelings to come in the middle of the genuine bond and understanding we share. He is undoubtedly an incredible man inside and out, and I love him for it. In fact, apart from love, I have massive respect for him too. He made my and my friends' nights over and again and had a huge hand in making the last few years of my dancing career worth writing about. After all, he was one of those one-in-a-million men you get the privilege of coming across.

Chapter 8: My Affair

After finding a genuine friend in April, I started making more friends. I would go out every Sunday evening to a popular Hip Hop Club named Travis with a girl from work, and she introduced me to a guy who played basketball. However, that new guy and I immediately started hanging out a lot, and he was also a lot of fun to go out with. In fact, his entire personality was very fun-loving, and he knew how to have a good time. Soon it started to become an every night thing. I would go to work early, get off at 11 or 12 and go out with him to clubs.

My friend Laura would leave work every night and go to clubs with him. I always glammed up for work, so I was always ready. I believed in making an impression and maintaining it. I never went to work in sweatpants or house shoes, unlike a lot of other girls. In fact, I dressed to impress every time I left home. I have always been someone who likes to look neat, clean, and presentable. For a while, things were fine, but I started getting drained from going out so much, working out during the day, working at nightclubs till

12 am, going to clubs with him, staying with him, and getting up early to get home to my dogs. Needless to say, my whole schedule was off.

My best friend Laura and I

Additionally, the guy I was hanging out with had some things going on in his life that I didn't know about. He sold his huge home in Highland Park, got dropped from a team, and started drinking every night. I wasn't a drinker, so I mostly drove us. Drinking and drugs were a common practice in the industry I belong to. Once, he also got arrested for drinking, which wasn't a good situation. Not to mention, he always asked me for money and would even leave clubs without paying his tabs, and it started to reflect badly on me. After all, I had a certain image and reputation. Intentionally, I wasn't willing to compromise on that, but things escalated too quickly for me to process.

Surely, he was going through a tough phase, if that's what you call it. It turned out that I was helping him to the point that I was hurting myself. Sometimes, you're so deep into a situation that you fail to realize how toxic it is for you, and the same happened to me. Anyways, this went on for a few years, and from time to time, his ex-teammate would come to town, and we would go out and club. He would have a different girl with him every time, but for some reason, he never wanted me to talk to him. He always seemed very protective of me when he would come around.

However, one night at dinner, I made eye contact with him, and it was simply outstanding. During that time, he was actually with a girlfriend of mine, but there was no connection between them. Their interactions seemed dull, dry, and boring. On the other hand, we couldn't stop staring at each other. Throughout the night, he and I continued to make eye contact with each other. I couldn't believe it because I was so respectful to D, no matter who was hitting on me.

Years passed, and D was just too much for me to deal with. There was a point where I decided it was enough and no longer wanted to be with him. Thus, I broke it off and moved on with my life. By now, I was living in Frisco and had a best friend named Laura. I had become so close to her, she was always staying over, and she was my ride-or-die. Not to mention, we hustled together and hung out together. It all dates back to how she and I met at a friend's birthday, and we instantly hit it off.

My best friend Laura and I

On a Wednesday night, we went to a nightclub called Candleroom. When I walked in, two seven-foot guys were standing just inside the door when I walked in. It was D and his friend Vamp. Although D and I still spoke, everything between us was over, but I spoke to both. Vamp grabbed my hand, but I kept walking out. The next day, Vamp got my number through a mutual friend and called me.

That night, we had dinner at Kenny's in Addison, TX, close to the house he still had in town from when he lived here and played ball. We enjoyed a wonderful dinner together, and there's no denying that there was so much chemistry. In fact, our energies were so in sync. After dinner, I drove him home and went home too. I didn't expect it, but the next night, we met again and went to a club together. Later on, we went to his place, and after some talking, he joked about how tense his shoulders were. I guess he was trying to get flirty.

I remember joking and telling him how I gave the best massages ever. Therefore, when we pulled up to his house, he asked if I wanted to come in, to which I replied saying, "I better not, and I'll catch you next time." All of this happened in April, and he was back in town in June. Once again, we met, went out for dinner, and went back to his house. Since he had a massage table, I agreed to give him one, and in return, he gave me one too.

This was the very night that it all started; our connection was like no other. We were shooting fireworks that could be spotted from a mile away. At this time, I had an apartment that was not too far away from his home. I was preparing to quit dancing in a year while building up the place I had just purchased in the country. On his visit, he ended up staying for two weeks. We hardly left his house and just couldn't get enough of each other. In fact, if onlookers were to comment on us, they would say something like us being in the initial stages of a new relationship when the couple is all lovey-dovey. Now that I think about it, we really had something special going on.

When it was time for him to go, I had a bittersweet feeling. I had missed two weeks of work and needed to get back in the game, but I knew I would miss him like crazy. After all, I was so attached to him, and it would take a few days to get back into my normal routine. We would talk the whole time, even when he was on his six-hour drive back to his hometown. We were just inseparable. This one time, I remember asking him if he had a girl back home since that is something he didn’t talk about for the two weeks we spent together.

Given our closeness, I felt like I had the right to ask and know. I was curious and wanted to know my place in his life. When we were together, we didn't leave each other's side, he wasn't on the phone at all, and I had no reason to suspect anything. Anyways, he told me that he had two nannies for his kids, so I thought he was single. Shortly after, there was an odd silence, and then I laughed, saying, "What do you have a wife or something?" Once again, there was an unpleasant silence. By this time, my thoughts started running wild; I told him to answer and not lie about anything. What I heard next was something I wasn't prepared for, and the news had me shocked; he finally replied, saying yes.

Naturally, I was taken aback and didn't know what to say except that I'll talk to him later. An hour or so passed, and he called me, and I straight up told him that I couldn't believe how he kept that hidden from me. He said he would be back in town the following week, and we would talk about everything. Despite our last conversation, our connection grew stronger. The following week when he returned, there was little talk about his home life. Nevertheless, we were connected every second. He stayed in town for a few weeks, and since his house was only a few miles away from my apartment, there was constant back and forth. I was also ensuring to take care of my dogs.

During this time, I was in my last year of dancing and was doing some final touches on my property because I was set to move in January 2017. Toward the end of 2016, he was very supportive in helping me shift; our relationship was still intact, the feelings were definitely far stronger, and the sexual chemistry was undeniable. I had never trusted any man in such a manner. We had something very mind-blowing; we did everything together, we went on road trips, spent time at his Miami house, and he would also take me to visit my sister in work release down in Ft. Lauderdale.

I just let him decide when he wanted to talk to me about his life. However, he didn't do it as often as he should have. Another thing I noticed was how he never took calls from his home, no one was calling, so I didn't know what to ask. It seemed as if he was disconnected from his house since how could no one wonder where he was when so much time had passed?

Me and my sister

In December 2016, I injured my shoulder at the gym. I had been going to a sports therapy center. One day I was adjusted by a chiropractor and had an injury. He manipulated my neck, and I was instantly dizzy and suffered double vision. I was alone, it was close to Christmas, and I was set to fly home to Florida. Vamp was not in Dallas at this time, but my good friend Dave met me at the hospital, where I went into testing. Since I was so scared, the doctors suggested I cancel my flight.

Vamp came to town and was kind enough to help me move to my new property and get settled in. Moreover, he also surprised me with a puppy he brought from Mississippi, and we named her Angel. She was such an adorable, friendly and obedient little puppy. I loved playing and cuddling with her. Luckily, I still have her today. Vamp helped me a lot, but I still had to go to Dallas on the weekend to dance. He gave me the key to his house, so I didn't drive home at night. Things went on for the next year, and finally, I was done dancing. But, little did I know that trouble was on its way. Unfortunately, someone was keeping a very close eye on us and demanded money from him not to talk.

Me and my dog Angel

We were both shocked and scared. His friends knew about me, and my friends knew about him. The guard gate lady used to give me a hard time when I would come in.

Despite having a pass on my car, she would stop me and ask me questions. Due to this, I was certain she was friends with someone in his family, and they were building a story against me. As crazy as it may sound, he just paid off my land, and all this started happening.

I couldn't see life without him, and we were both finding it hard to let go. Six weeks had passed, and we were only talking on the phone. I had started working for a fast-paced delivery company delivering packages.I was working 50-plus hours. He would call on my way to work, and I would cry. One day, I finally gathered the courage and told him we needed to stop this interaction. I suggested how it's better to move on gracefully. Even though I made my point clear, months passed, and he would still call daily to the point that I could no longer hear his voice because of the hurt.

I was distracted and also found it hard to focus on work. Then one night, I called his wife and told her to make Vamp stop calling me. She was completely shocked to hear about the last several years; I didn't say a lot since I didn't feel the need to. However, I did feel bad about having to break the news to her. While I don't know her place in his life, I can only imagine how she must've felt hearing about her husband through another woman.

We spoke for about ten minutes, and I questioned her if she did not wonder where he was all this time. To my surprise, she didn't seem to know but said that the pieces of the puzzle were now fitting. Just as I thought, he never called me again, allowing me to move on and see myself. However, not a day passes that I don't think about him. As a matter of fact, three years have passed, and I have not dated or touched another man. I love who I am, and I am at a point where I can say that I have experienced everything. I have learned from my mistakes; being single and working on myself has brought me to a place where I will not risk over a man until it's the real thing. Now, will that ever happen? I don't know.

But I do know that I am a much better woman. And even though I never ever asked him about his home life, I knew. He and I never argued about anything. He was 100% there for me, and I never had a love and connection for anyone like I did with him. It's something that I can't really put into words. The way he looked at me was a way that I had never been looked at before. We would hug each other. Moreover, we were always so excited to see each other and spend some good quality time. For so many years, we only had a few arguments.

We just didn't spend our time arguing about anything because the love between us was too precious to be wasted on trivial things. In case we had a disagreement, we talked it out and moved on. Although, the last year was hard for both of us. We struggled to let go and had to deal with so much pain. Sometimes, I miss him and all the comfort I had with him.

But there are times in your life when you have to let go of the past and make healthier choices. Don't get me wrong; I'm not implying he was toxic. It's just that we had an excellent run, but up to a certain point, we had to go our own separate ways. And that's okay. I still have love and respect for him and wish him well from the bottom of my heart.

Chapter 9: Looking Back

As I look back and reflect on my life, I'm proud to say that I don't have a single regret. In fact, I believe regrets are stupid because why regret something you once wanted or enjoyed? Life is too short to waste time feeling sad or sorry for what happened in the past. Life is always what you choose to make of it, so choose happiness, growth, and peace. A lot of people tend to ask me if I regret all those years in the club, and my answer has always been no. There's absolutely no denying that the clubs were a huge stepping stone for me to get to where I am today.

Looking back on that day working at Hooters when I was eighteen and burning through a million dollars, it seems surreal. If I didn't live that life, I wouldn't believe it. Fortunately, I helped so many people without even thinking about it, and I already had an unbelievable life before dancing. So, I wasn't shocked by anything and remained humble. My entire life, I've seen numerous girls struggle with drug abuse, overdose, and even lose their kids.

Despite the fact that some went to college, nursing school, and law school, they were still unhappy. Personally, I feel like your choices define you and shape and influence your life to a great extent. The choices those girls made were mostly on the basis of either short-term instant gratification or were ill-planned and not in life with their futures. I, on the other hand, was driven and highly motivated to unlock the keys to success. As a result, I stayed in control of my life, looked passed judgments, and never had to lie to my parents about what I did. Not to mention, I also managed to successfully block my childhood out.

After all, it's essential to remember the positive things and focus on the good because that's what keeps you going. Luckily, I have a relationship with both my parents, even though I lost my stepdad years ago. But you know, losing someone doesn't mean you stop thinking about them or loving them. As a matter of fact, I want to point out that it was him who I owe the most to. I wish he was here to read this book; nevertheless, I'm certain that he's up there smiling and is super proud of me. I find myself to be so lucky because my entire life went exactly as planned.

Very few people get the privilege of living life on their own terms, and I was one of those lucky ones. I know most people will say I could've done life differently, but honestly, I can't picture it going any other way. I have everything I've ever wanted; a ranch with amazing horses and all the dogs a girl could ever want. I turned my love for dogs into a dream. I carefully bypassed several paths that could've landed me in places that I would've never been able to share with you. A huge part of me feels like I was chosen for this life.

I met some lovely people who blessed my life, and in return, I blessed the lives of others. Life has been full of twists and turns, but I coped with everything and kept my face toward the sunshine. Unfortunately, my sister is in prison again and is serving what I hope is her last time there. I'm filled with intense emotions and tears as I pen this down. She has five more years; I miss her terribly, and she deserves all the happiness in the world because she got me out of that house at sixteen. If it wasn't for her, I wouldn't have made it so far. Undeniably my sister has played a key role in changing my life, and I hold that memory super close to my heart.

As for my career, I was highly focused and blocked out all the extra noise around me. I outdanced all the girls I knew in this business and made my way to the top like no other. The point to be noted is when I started dancing back in 1999, the stage was set for failure from every direction. It was up to me to pave my own path from the first few months in the club, and being with a pimp is what opened my eyes to the reality of this industry and how things work. In all honesty, the leader in me and my eye for detail is what allowed me to make it. Now, let me talk about pimps.

April and I

Pimps that work with girls in the club are different from street pumps. Also, pimps that work in the club seek out girls from places like malls and restaurants as waitresses or regular jobs, if you know what I mean. The girls who are struck with these probably show up in the latest Benz, Range Rover, or Bentleys. These cars are usually in the main girl's name (bottom girl), the girl who has been with them the longest. These pimps pick girls according to their potential, which means they can take them to the salon and groom them.

Elizabeth, April, and I

By category, these are the classiest pimps that have the prettiest girls in the club and drive the nicest cars, and more girls are drawn to them. In my case, it was all in, so allow me to explain. Every night you handed a lot of money over, you had one day off weekly, and if you went in early and made $1k, you could go out for a night with the pimp mostly to scout girls.

Due to this, the girls thought the pimp was making my money work for me. However, the truth was that I stepped up my platform on his game before I ever stepped into a club. You see, I already blew a million dollars, so he wasn't treating me to anything new. In fact, I was turning him onto things. I had a presidential Rolex, jewelry, cars, and all that before any other girl in the club. Nevertheless, we were an item, and I respected the game. I didn't disrespect him for two years. Together, we got money, girls, and whatever we wanted. He would willingly send me to Memphis, Miami, and wherever.

Not to mention, I would come back with a big stack of money. After a few years, I broke loose, it wasn't easy to remember, and I was the source of the look. Guys and girls had to make a certain amount in order to be on our team. You could not drink in the clubs or smoke, and trust me, if you did, someone would tell him. I still remember once a girl came along and decided to smoke one night in the club. So, another pimp that was in the club saw her and called TC. After she got off work, he asked her to light up a cigarette, and when she did, he made her chew and swallow it along with a $100 bill.

The aftermath was that she didn't stay around, and neither could she get a job at any of the hot spots. Coming back to me leaving, he went out of town to take another girl to work, and I planned it all out a few weeks prior. So, I had already rented an apartment, and my manager allowed me to stack money in the safe to prepare for the night. The other girl who was with TC before, I got with him and wanted to leave. Also, I want to mention that she was not as strong as me; she did drugs on the side, and neither did she make as much money.

However, she was really pretty, loyal, came from a good family, dressed well, and drove a convertible Mercedes. She served as an inspiration for other girls to also look at their part and live a life as great as hers. So about her and me, I didn't go home, and he was constantly blowing up both of our phones. He was all she knew, and he met her on a sidewalk years ago and put her in the clubs, but she did leave. We avoided the clubs for a few nights even though I had to pay a supervisor $1k to keep him off the property. Fortunately, at that point, I had everyone in my pocket in the clubs. Money talks, and a few months passed, and I was doing my thing. Once that girl got her freedom, she didn't continue dancing.

Instead, she started partying a lot, got into drugs, and went down a bad road. Anyways, looking back on those days and all that I was, I even took bad situations and turned them into stepping stones. The thing is, not all girls who had pimps made it out so lucky, but since I knew the control and power I had with what I was doing. The pimps would come at the until they saw I was not playing that game, but they still wanted me to be on their team because of my knowledge. They would tell their girls not to talk to me at work since they knew I had a history with a pimp in Florida. Additionally, they also knew I pulled his girls away when I left, and I was recognized as the million-dollar girl.

Despite the fact that they knew I would not give up my money, they still wanted to try. This reminds me of two girls in particular that were in Dallas. Those girls worked seven days a week; they were pretty classy and were being sold a dream by this pimp. I remember watching them closely in the clubs and the way they moved around. One of those girls was quite similar to me, and although we wanted to talk to each other, there were too many eyes around. So, for four years, I watched them every single night, and I knew they were making big money and giving it to this pimp who was clearly lying to them and giving them a big life.

One night, I randomly got a message on a social platform, and she said, "Summer, I need your help. I want to leave, and I'm scared." After seeing that text, my only question was, "When do you want to leave?" to which she replied, "Tomorrow." I then asked her to share the address; I rented a u haul and called my good friend Dave to get things rolling. He and I devised a plan and headed to her given address the next day. Soon as we pulled him, we quickly covered all the cameras with towels and started loading her up. She had secured an apartment in a really nice area.

Now, this is the same girl who worked for seven nights a week for seven years and made probably a million easily and was giving it all to this guy. Unfortunately, she left with no car, and her life wasn't ideal. She got the chance to drive fancy cars like a Range Rover, but nothing was in her name. Thus, she ended up with nothing. She had been so sheltered and was really scared, but we managed to get her out, and slowly she got back on top.

Currently, she lives in Vegas and is working on several new businesses, getting out of that industry and helping other girls. But let me explain the severe trauma that comes along with the life she was living. Her social skills had to be reinvented; all she knew was hustling in the clubs and making money. To top off things, she wasn't allowed to see other girls, socialize or have a normal life. The things she told me about what he made her do to him were awful. But that's just one story; there are so many to be told about other girls and pimps in the club. So, trust me when I say that only the real ones survive; I really mean it. I went on twenty years in the club after being with a pimp.

In my first two years, no matter what state I was in, I had the reputation of being with a pimp and a girl who was given a million dollars. The good part was that the pimps knew I wasn't afraid, and I was the one with money, and I didn't hurt my lifestyle to throw a thousand down to a manager of the club to keep them down. I was way smarter than the other girls and was never a target for the pimps. In fact, I used to get offers from them to talk to other girls (usually the new ones) and try to get them to go with the pimps.

Girls would always look up to me, and I was walking proof you didn't need to work for anyone. I'm so grateful for so many things in life. My sister Jessica changed my path from that night years ago, and everything I say in appreciation for her is nothing compared to what she did for me. I never had drama, I helped people when I could, I had goals/dreams, and regardless of what I was doing, I was making money.

Money is what gives you endless options. Apart from that, I'm thankful for my family and that we were able to stick together. We faced difficulties and heartaches and always stood by each other. My mom lives in Texas close to me, and my dad is still someone I look up to. My maternal aunts have also always been there, and while we wait for my sister's sentence to be over, I'll continue to live my life to the fullest.

Chapter 10: Priceless Lessons

Life has been one hell of a crazy ride full of ups and downs, growth, success, fame, and, most importantly, learning. Learning is a life-long process and only stops the day you die. Undoubtedly, life has taught me a lot. Each phase of my life was different than the other, and as I look back to reflect, I wouldn't have had it any other way. I've learned some valuable lessons in my life that have influenced and shaped me. There's beauty in the madness.

There's a certain adventure in knowing the unknown. There's a thrill in chasing your dreams and living fearlessly. Personally, I believe each one of us has been destined for greatness and was born to shine. Thus, don't let anyone tell you that your dreams can't become a reality or that you don't have what it takes. It doesn't matter where you're coming from or what your background or appearance is.

Remember, you have a story to tell, a voice that needs to be heard, a passion for living, and dreams to transform into reality. And those are reasons enough. Life is really short, don't let it surpass you. Make each day of your life count. Life to the fullest and worry less. I know some of these things are easier said than done but take it from me. I had no idea how my life would pan out when I was a kid. Nevertheless, I made good use of my mind, time, and resources. I acted when the iron was hot, and look where I am today. Life is also about choices, and the choices we make define us to a great extent.

Back then, I took some risks and survived some challenging situations. I had the courage to persist and keep pushing forward. Of course, it's different for everyone. But all I want you to know in your heart with certainty is that you, too, have the potential and capability to do whatever you aspire to do. The idea that you have in your head execute it. The risk you're scared to take, take it. The goal you want to attain, work toward it. For the person you love, let them know your feelings. From my personal experiences, I will tell you to live every single day of your life as if it's your last. And no, I don't mean to say live it recklessly.

Instead, live it mindfully and make your life a collection of beautiful memories you can cherish and proudly look back on. Many people ask me what is the craziest thing that has ever happened to me. Well, to tell you the truth, I've experienced several crazy things, but one stands out. One night in Miami, at a club named "Scarlett's Cabaret," a man had been giving me 100's on stage. We talked for some time, and I happened to mention that I was only in town for a week. I explained that I was taking Ubers to and from work. Mind you, I had no intention of making him give me anything.

I was just casually sharing a piece of information while we interacted. Toward the end of the night, when I was doing my last stage set, he walked by and tossed a shiny car key. Those keys weren't just any keys; they were for a two-door convertible Bentley. I almost couldn't believe it, and naturally, my jaw dropped in amazement. Soon as I got off stage, my eyes searched for him, but he was nowhere to be found. I then went to the management of the club and informed them about receiving car keys for a man as that was the responsible thing to do. Anyways, we went outside, and

I saw a brand-new Bentley waiting for me. A note on the front seat said, "Enjoy your week in Miami and use my car. I'll be back in a week. See you."

He also left 70000 under the note and instructed me to pay for my hotel with that money. I was at a loss for words and did exactly as I was instructed. It may not speak to everyone, but this particular story really speaks to me. If I talk about right now, I want to continue my life rescuing dogs, building a beautiful pet hotel, riding/training horses, barrel racing, and doing all the things that make me happy. Simultaneously, I hope to have things set up for my sister when she comes home. There are days when I feel so tired, but she keeps me wanting to do better.

I have accomplished so much, and I'm not stopping there. I am grateful for the relationship I have with my parents. They've been good. I don't spend enough time with my family in Florida, but I want to change that, and I believe I can. My sister's kids are really important to me, and her oldest has three kids that are simply precious. My fast-paced lifestyle brought a lot of memories, but the ones with family are different in a good way. As I went through the journey of life, I learned that you can't trust everyone you meet.

Me and some of my dogs at my ranch

As a matter of fact, not everyone is worth your trust, either. Additionally, in some situations, trust can even get you killed. I've never had a large group of friends; I did a lot of things alone and was completely fine with that. Being able to spend time by yourself is also an art not many people are familiar with or can master. Coming back to friends, after all these years, there are four of them that I've been close to for over twenty years.

My childhood friends Heather, Leslie, Lisa, and Tiffany, are absolute gems. I am pretty sure that if I ever needed them, they would be here. It has taken me a while, but I now understand the true meaning of quality over quantity. I know we all have had a life not too many could understand, including mine. I have most certainly made some mistakes, just like everyone else. I've laid down plenty of nights not being proud of the things I've done. Nevertheless, I've learned from my mistakes and tried to be better each time. I have said it over and over, and I'll say it again, the clubs gave me freedom and allowed me to be free. I felt free in the sense of not slowing down and unapologetically loving myself from the inside out.

I got the chance to love myself, and that was something I missed doing. And now, that's something I'm learning. Honestly, it feels good to know your worth and own it. It took me some events in life to get to where I am, but I'm happy now. I've come to realize that when you truly love yourself, people can't break you. You become a tough nut to crack, and the barrier of self-love is high enough not to let toxic, unnecessary, or negative people close to you. I've lived a life most will only read or watch about on TV.

So, life's small, petty things don't affect me at all. I'm living for Summer now and my sister, her kids, and my parents. I can count on these people as they won't let me down. I was never asked why I did something, and from time to time, my dad would say he was proud of me. The power in those words is something I can't explain. If I were to pass on a message to the youth, I would ask them to chase their dreams and remember that it's never too late.

Your dreams are not going to fall in your lap. You need to work hard and find a way to do what you love. Another thing I want to point out is that your passion, thirst to prove yourself, and random acts of kindness do not go unnoticed. Life will pass us by so quickly. We are all so unique, and there is a passion in all of us. Before I end this, I want to share something that a family told me years ago when I was going through a divorce and didn't know where life was headed.

Enjoying life at the Brenner Ranch with late dog Elizabeth and horse "Get Drunk and Trashy."

In 2007 I met some great people, which were the Brenners, in Sulphur Springs, TX. I met them through my ex-husband, and they train cutting horses. To this day, I look up to them as family. But, one evening, I was at their place, and just before I left, Mr. Brenner said, "Summer, our door is always open for you. Put your horses in the barn and come inside. We won't ask a thing." These words left a huge imprint on me and filled my heart with gratitude. I still tear up; just recalling that dialogue and writing it now makes me so emotional. He truly meant it, and I didn't hear a lot of true words like that my whole life, and I will take it with me forever.

And one last thing to lighten the mood I'd like to end this book by saying that laughter really is the medicine for everything. I have the greatest laughter with my mom over the years, sharing stories over the phone after work about things that happened. We find a way to laugh and smile about something each day. So, my advice to you is to laugh and laugh as much as you can. Find joy in the little things, and one day when you look back, you will realize that they weren't little.

Remember, you only get to live once, and if you do it right, then once really is enough. Finally, here's me wishing you love, light, and guidance for you to maneuver through the course of life. I'm confident that you will find your way, similar to how I found mine. This is your moment, so own it!

Made in the USA
Columbia, SC
05 December 2024

48431157R00072